Contents

Official Annual

WE DARE YOU!

OK. Here it is...the Official World Wrestling Federation Annual No. 3! All your favorite Superstars are in the action, in the air and in your face! Come inside and meet heroic Hulk, the unearthly Undertaker and Giant Gonzalez, who simply beggars the imagination.

Turn the page...
WE DARE YOU!

Publisher & Editor-in-Chief: **Thomas H.W. Emanuel** • Executive Editor: **Edward R. Ricciuti** • Staff Writer: **Lou Gianfriddo** • Design: **JAT Associates** • Photography Director: **Stephen H. Taylor** • Staff Photographer: **Tom Buchanan** • Production Director: **Alina L. Massaro** • Photo Editors: **Marybeth Marrion, Suzanne Pullen** • Copy Editor: **Midge Bacon** • Typesetting Manager: **Linda L. Nishball** • Puzzles: **Larry Humber** • Special thanks to: **Matt Kornhass, Troy Santi, Tricia Breheney**

Published by Grandreams Limited, Jadwin House, 205/211 Kentish Town Road, London, NW5 2JU Printed in Italy.
ISBN 0 85830 057 6

Bret The "Hit Man"

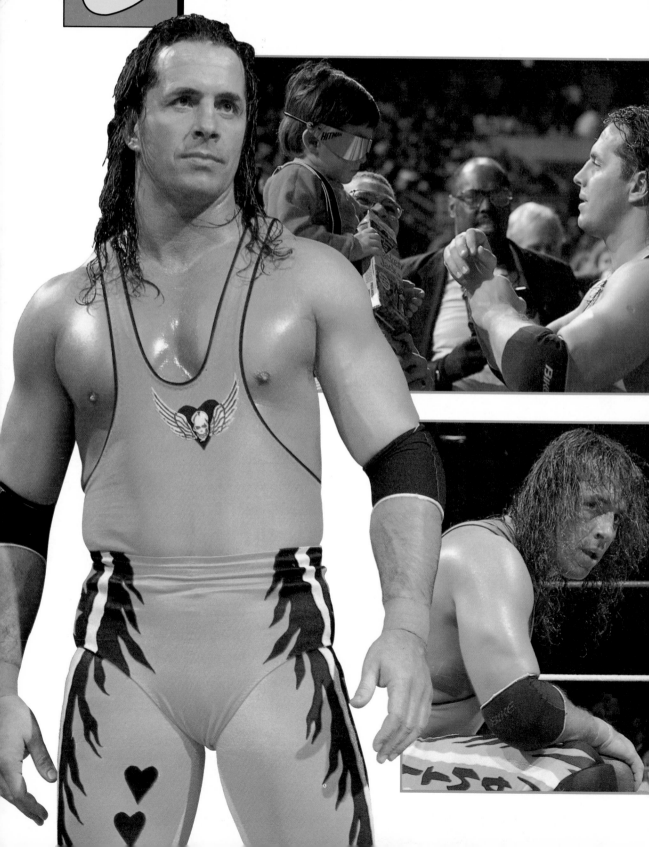

Hart*

B ret "Hit Man" Hart will always remember October 11, 1992—and not just because it is Canada's Thanksgiving Day. On that day, the young native of Calgary, Alberta, Canada, stepped into the ring and took the World Wrestling Federation Title from Ric Flair. Most fittingly, the win took place in Saskatoon, Saskatchewan, which like Alberta is one of Canada's western provinces. Better yet, Bret's entire family, including his father, former

ring great Stu Hart, was in the audience.

"It was a dream come true," says Bret. "But who ever would have dreamed I would win the title with my family there? It was incredible. I'll always remember it."

The victory was made even sweeter following what had happened at *SummerSlam*, which occurred in the United Kingdom's Wembley Stadium. The Hit Man went into the squared circle to defend his World Wrestling Federation Intercontinental Championship against his brother-in-law, the British Bulldog—and lost. But he didn't lose heart.

After winning the title, Bret became a fighting champion, taking on the likes of Papa Shango, Virgil, Razor Ramon and Shawn Michaels.

At *WrestleMania IX*, Bret lost the title to Yokozuna due to interference by Mr. Fuji. Only seconds later, Yokozuna fell to Hulk Hogan.

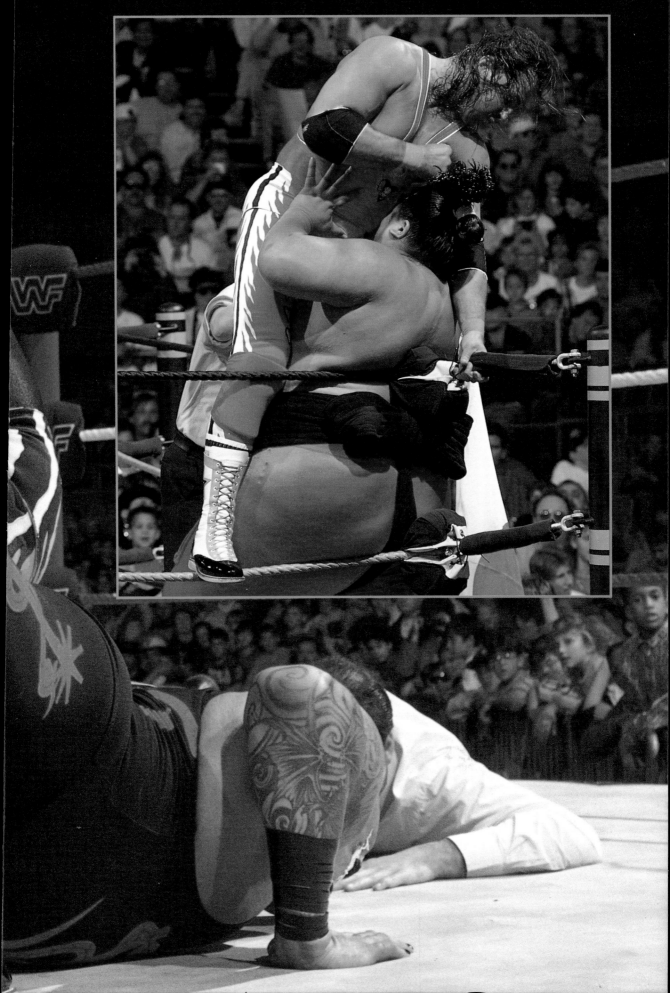

Yokozuna*

His name means the Grand Champion of Japanese sumo wrestling. From the South Pacific, Yokozuna conquered Japan, just as this 505-pound leviathan is now conquering the World Wrestling Federation. Even the feared Undertaker felt his wrath.

Managed by Mr. Fuji, Yokozuna combines huge size, knowledge of sumo power moves and experience in the martial arts to overwhelm his opponents.

Yokozuna has the dubious distinction of holding the World Wrestling Federation Championship for mere minutes. At *WrestleMania IX*, he took it from Bret Hart, then immediately challenged Hulk Hogan. Moments later a trick by Fuji backfired, and Hogan won the belt.

Tatanka*

Sporting an undefeated record in the World Wrestling Federation, the exciting Native American Tatanka exploded into the *Survivor Series* with a vengeance. His opponent was the Model Rick Martel, who had stolen Tatanka's sacred eagle feathers.

Tatanka, who has overcome one worthy opponent after another, tore into Martel, whipped him and came away with his pride—and precious feathers.

At *WrestleMania IX* Tatanka beat reigning Intercontinental champ Shawn Michaels, but by a count-out. Under Federation rules, however, the title cannot change hands via a count-out.

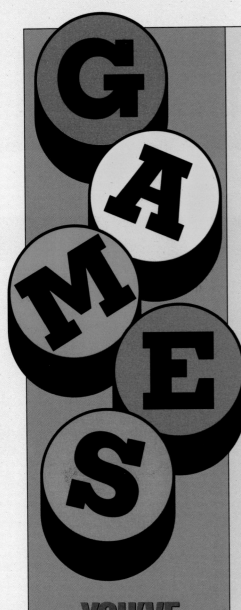

GAMES

YOU'VE REALLY GOT A HOLD ON ME

Pictured are a dozen World Wrestling Federation superstars. Alongside are the finishing moves they've made famous. Each move is missing a couple of letters, though. First, fill in the missing letters. Then, try to match each superstar with his favorite finisher.

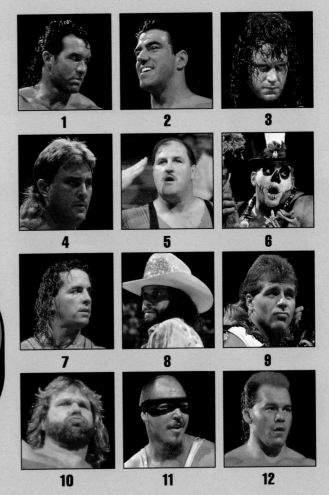

1   2   3

4   5   6

7   8   9

10   11   12

#__ B__CK S__PL__X

#__ SH__RPSH__ __T__R

#__ R__NN__NG CL__TH__SL__N__

#__ CR__N__ __M CR__NCH

#__ R__V__RS__ F__LL__W__Y SL__M

#__ SH__ __LD__RBR__ __K__R

#__ B__ST__N CR__B

#__ CR__WB__R L__G GR__P__V__N__

#__ C__BR__ CL__TCH

#__ F__LL__W__Y SL__M

#__ __LB__W __FF TH__ T__P R__P__S

#__ T__MBST__N__

Razor Ramon*

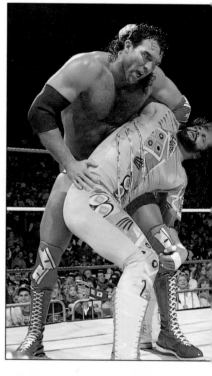

Big and burly Razor Ramon, who left Cuba for Miami, Florida, under clouded circumstances, has established himself as one of the most vicious men in the World Wrestling Federation. Razor says that he came to the United States to take what he wants—and he wants it all.

"Hey, hey, chico," sneers Razor, "some fools from my country came to the States to work, but I come here, and I just grab it all."

Razor should be known by the company he keeps, including Ric Flair and sleazy Bobby "The Brain" Heenan. He teamed with Flair against Mr. Perfect and Macho Man Randy Savage at the *Survivor Series*. Razor and his pal were so unsportsmanlike that they were disqualified. That time, however, Razor didn't get what he wanted. He went home in defeat.

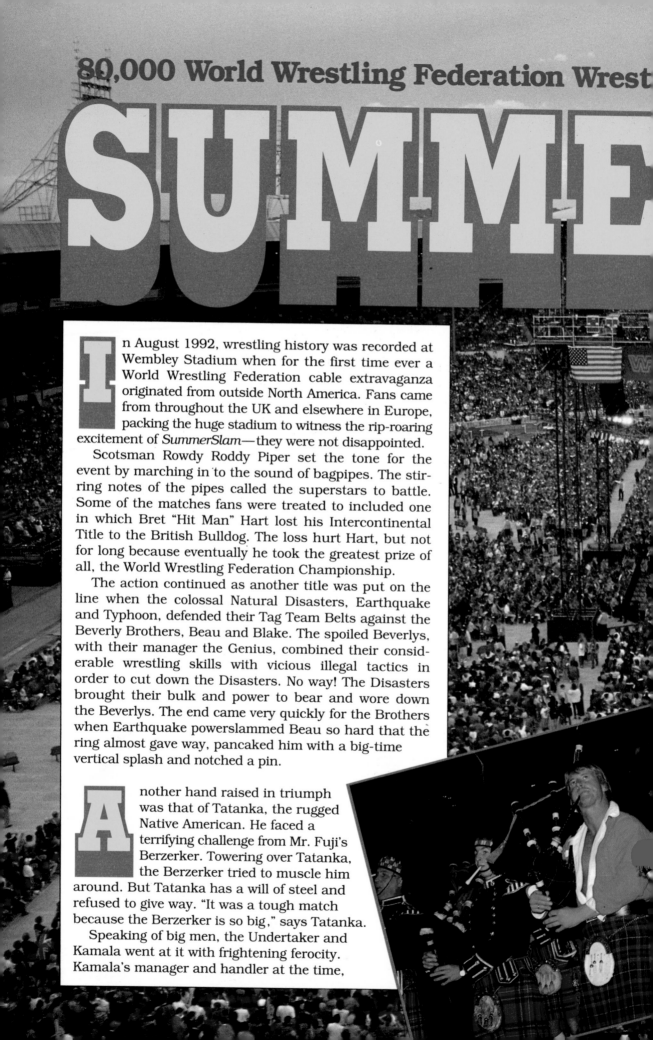

SUMME

In August 1992, wrestling history was recorded at Wembley Stadium when for the first time ever a World Wrestling Federation cable extravaganza originated from outside North America. Fans came from throughout the UK and elsewhere in Europe, packing the huge stadium to witness the rip-roaring excitement of *SummerSlam*—they were not disappointed.

Scotsman Rowdy Roddy Piper set the tone for the event by marching in to the sound of bagpipes. The stirring notes of the pipes called the superstars to battle. Some of the matches fans were treated to included one in which Bret "Hit Man" Hart lost his Intercontinental Title to the British Bulldog. The loss hurt Hart, but not for long because eventually he took the greatest prize of all, the World Wrestling Federation Championship.

The action continued as another title was put on the line when the colossal Natural Disasters, Earthquake and Typhoon, defended their Tag Team Belts against the Beverly Brothers, Beau and Blake. The spoiled Beverlys, with their manager the Genius, combined their considerable wrestling skills with vicious illegal tactics in order to cut down the Disasters. No way! The Disasters brought their bulk and power to bear and wore down the Beverlys. The end came very quickly for the Brothers when Earthquake powerslammed Beau so hard that the ring almost gave way, pancaked him with a big-time vertical splash and notched a pin.

Another hand raised in triumph was that of Tatanka, the rugged Native American. He faced a terrifying challenge from Mr. Fuji's Berzerker. Towering over Tatanka, the Berzerker tried to muscle him around. But Tatanka has a will of steel and refused to give way. "It was a tough match because the Berzerker is so big," says Tatanka.

Speaking of big men, the Undertaker and Kamala went at it with frightening ferocity. Kamala's manager and handler at the time,

aniacs Make Sizzling Grappling History!

RSLAM!*

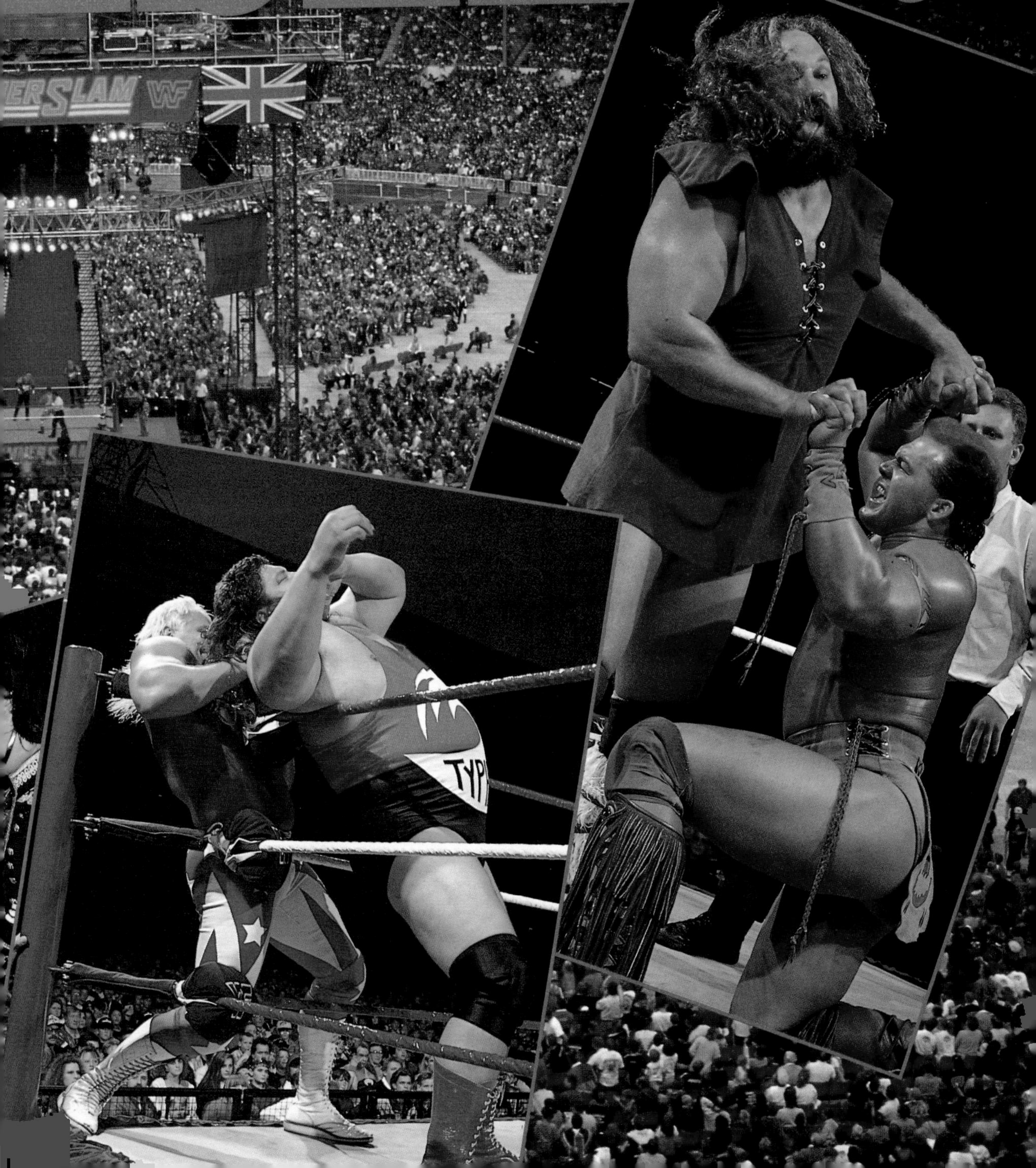

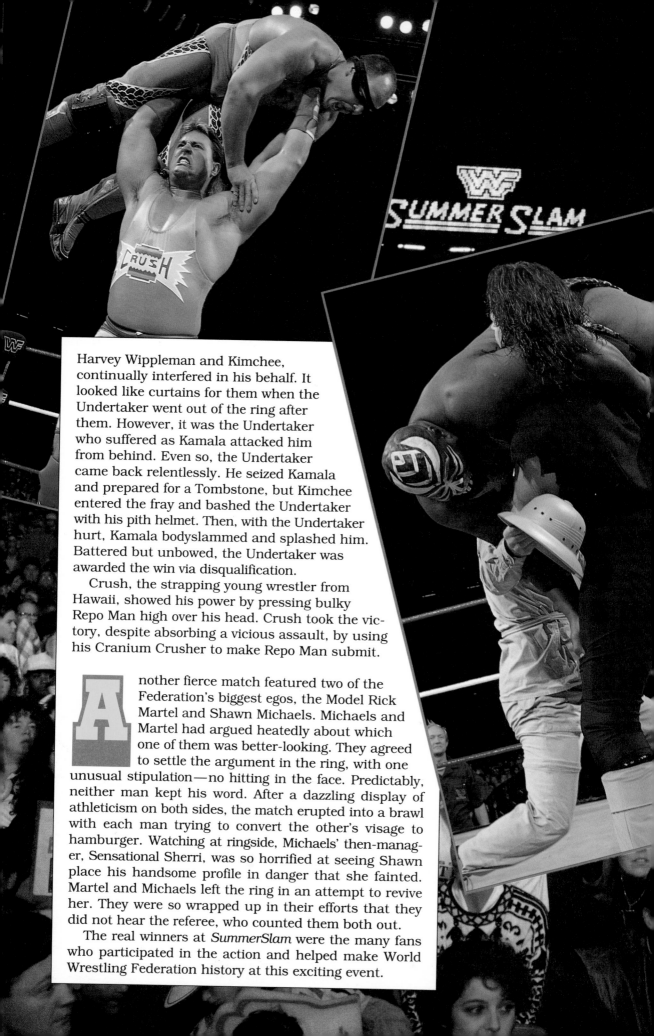

Harvey Wippleman and Kimchee, continually interfered in his behalf. It looked like curtains for them when the Undertaker went out of the ring after them. However, it was the Undertaker who suffered as Kamala attacked him from behind. Even so, the Undertaker came back relentlessly. He seized Kamala and prepared for a Tombstone, but Kimchee entered the fray and bashed the Undertaker with his pith helmet. Then, with the Undertaker hurt, Kamala bodyslammed and splashed him. Battered but unbowed, the Undertaker was awarded the win via disqualification.

Crush, the strapping young wrestler from Hawaii, showed his power by pressing bulky Repo Man high over his head. Crush took the victory, despite absorbing a vicious assault, by using his Cranium Crusher to make Repo Man submit.

Another fierce match featured two of the Federation's biggest egos, the Model Rick Martel and Shawn Michaels. Michaels and Martel had argued heatedly about which one of them was better-looking. They agreed to settle the argument in the ring, with one unusual stipulation—no hitting in the face. Predictably, neither man kept his word. After a dazzling display of athleticism on both sides, the match erupted into a brawl with each man trying to convert the other's visage to hamburger. Watching at ringside, Michaels' then-manager, Sensational Sherri, was so horrified at seeing Shawn place his handsome profile in danger that she fainted. Martel and Michaels left the ring in an attempt to revive her. They were so wrapped up in their efforts that they did not hear the referee, who counted them both out.

The real winners at *SummerSlam* were the many fans who participated in the action and helped make World Wrestling Federation history at this exciting event.

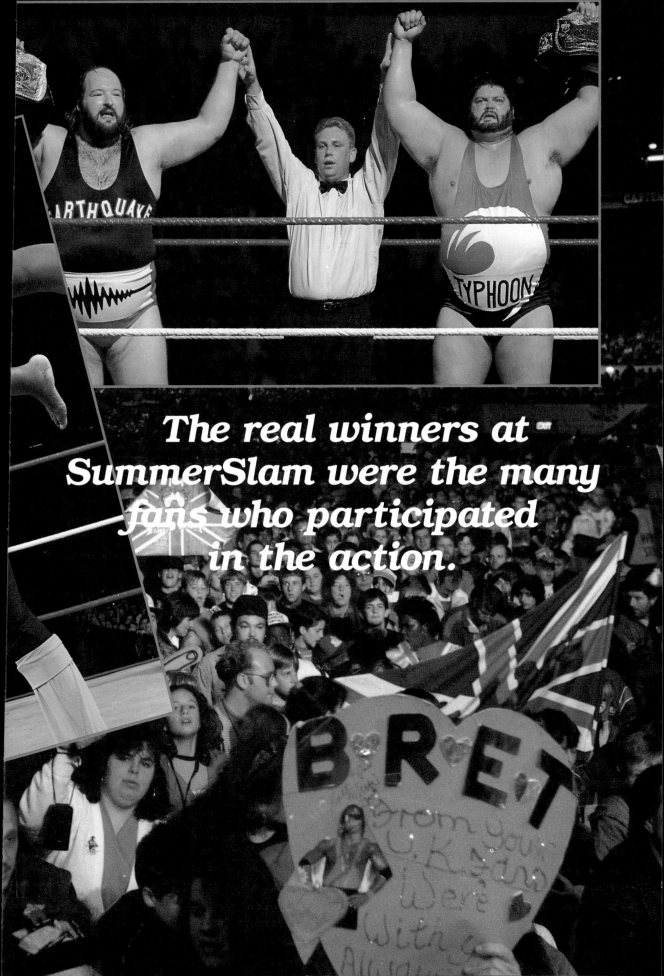

The real winners at SummerSlam were the many fans who participated in the action.

Crush*

C rush is the powerful Hawaiian who experts figure has a shining future in the World Wrestling Federation. This big, rugged wrestler acquired his name because, ever since he was a little boy, he has enjoyed crushing things.

Crush also learned that things are not always what they seem to be. He was ambushed by the evil Doink, who hit the Hawaiian with a fake arm that the not-so-funny clown had pretended was an injured limb.

Doink's treachery was at an all-time high when, at *WrestleMania IX*, he cruelly ambushed Crush again. Using a look-alike clown who had hidden under the ring, he double-teamed the Hawaiian and got the decision from a confused referee.

Bam Bam*

Big Bam Bam Bigelow returned to the World Wrestling Federation during the past year. He returned larger than ever and meaner than anyone has ever seen him. His goal was to win a title, no matter what it took. Thus, Bam Bam has been exceptionally ruthless, using his immense size and power to brutalize opponents.

They say Bam Bam was a professional bounty hunter at one time in his murky past, hunting down fugitives with methods not sanctioned by actual law enforcement officers. Now the bounty he hunts is gold. And his methods? Totally outside the World Wrestling Federation rulebook.

GAMES

OF MOUTH AND MEN

Jimmy "Mouth of the South" Hart is one of the World Wrestling Federation's most successful managers — his wrestlers have won numerous titles. Some of the champions with whom he's been involved are listed on the right, minus all of the consonants. It's up to you to fill them in. Once you've filled in all the missing letters, Hart's birthplace will appear in the boxed area (reading from the top).

```
        | O U _ _ I E
    _ _ | E _ _ A _ _
_ O _ _ Y _ O _ _| A _
        | Y _ _ O O _
    E A _ _ _| _ U A _ E
    _ _ _| I _ I A _ E
    _ _ _ O _|, and _ A _ _
```

The Undertaker*

He walks strange and eerie paths, this huge Undertaker, in the shadows of tombs and among the gravestones. With him goes his manager, Paul Bearer, holding the gold funeral urn from which the Undertaker derives his weird power.

The Undertaker had two crashing confrontations with Kamala the Ugandan Giant during the past year. In the first meeting, which was at *SummerSlam*, he was severely bashed by the apparently weighted pith helmet of Kamala's handler at the time, Kimchee. The decision was awarded to the Undertaker via disqualification of the Ugandan.

However, the Undertaker still had a score to settle with Kamala. At *Survivor Series*, he met Kamala again, beat him and then sealed him into a coffin.

The Undertaker, after being restored to consciousness by the power of the urn at *WrestleMania IX*, drove the towering Giant Gonzalez from the ring.

GAMES

BORN IN THE USA!

World Wrestling Federation superstars hail from across the U.S. and even Canada. See if you can match each of the pictured superstars with his hometown.

Calgary, Canada
—

Glens Falls, NY # —

Minneapolis, MN # —

Allentown, PA # —

Death Valley, CA
—

Shaker Heights, OH # —

Venice Beach, CA
—

Charlotte, NC
—

Norfolk, VA # —

San Antonio, TX # —

Sarasota, FL # —

Cobb County, GA # —

Repo Man*

Repo Man sneaks about, repossessing the personal possessions of people who find themselves unable to pay for them. He acts the same way in the ring, trying to repossess the hopes and dreams of his opponents in the World Wrestling Federation.

The slippery Repo Man is an extremely difficult foe, and his challengers never know how he will confront them. After defeating an opponent, Repo Man likes to hook the beaten man up to a tow-rope and haul him off.

The Narcissist Le

The Narcissist Lex Luger had his huge forearm "repaired" after an accident. Since that time, Luger has been knocking opponents cold with that same forearm. He even did it to Bret "Hit Man" Hart as Hart spoke during a special function before *WrestleMania IX*. "I was supposed to speak too, but when they cut me short because of Hart, that made me angry," explained Luger.

At *WrestleMania IX*, Luger took on Mr. Perfect. It was

Luger *

Luger's awesome power versus Perfect's spectacular skill. The referee ruled that Luger had pinned Perfect. Bad call! Perfect's feet were on the ropes.

Luger smirked about his victory after the event and vowed to smash all new challengers. We'll just wait to see.

Macho Man Randy

Savage*

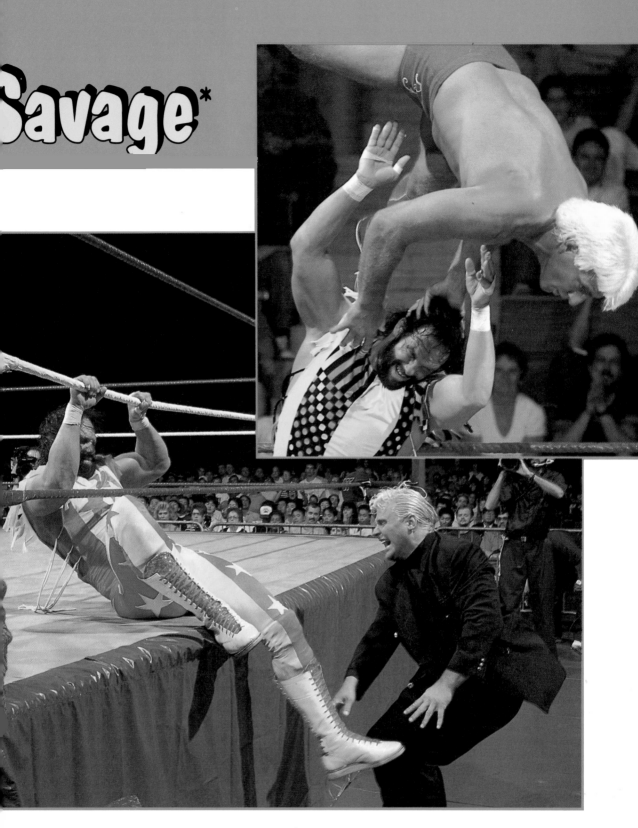

Macho Man Randy Savage defended his World Wrestling Federation Title against the Ultimate Warrior at *SummerSlam*. The thunderous match left him battered, his leg sorely injured. A short time later with his typical courage, he defended his belt against Ric Flair—and lost.

Savage ultimately gained revenge against Flair. The Macho Man needed a partner to wrestle both Flair and Razor Ramon at the *Survivor Series*. He challenged none other than Flair's very own Executive Consultant, Mr. Perfect, to team with him. To everyone's surprise, Perfect, sick of Flair, accepted. He and the Macho Man were victorious at the *Survivor Series* and won by means of a disqualification.

THE HULK HAS A HART!

THE IMMORTAL HULK HOGAN and Brutus "The Barber" Beefcake, under Jimmy "Mouth of the South" Hart's management, recently joined forces and are now known throughout the cosmos as the Mega-Maniacs. Hulkster and Beefcake have been lifelong friends, thus cementing the dynasty of this overwhelming combination for years to come. Turn the page to see what led to this fantastic team.

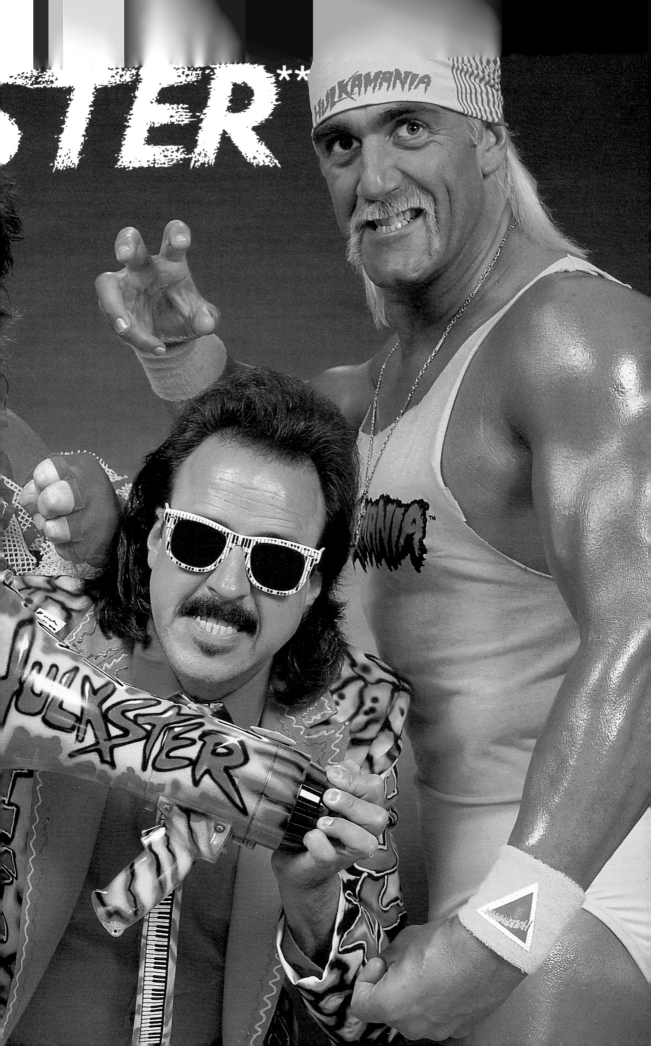

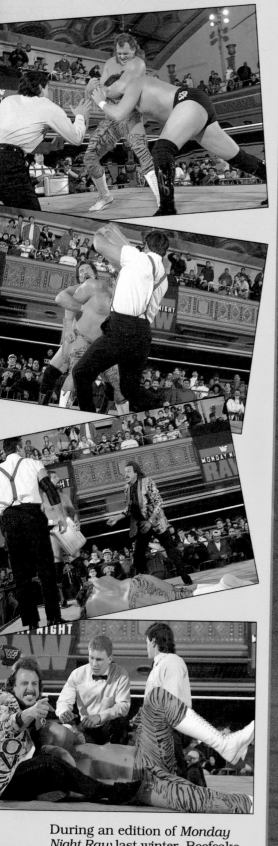

During an edition of *Monday Night Raw* last winter, Beefcake—who had just returned to the World Wrestling Federation after recovering from a near-fatal parasailing mishap in 1990—was Pearl Harbored by tag team Money Inc. Jimmy Hart, who managed Money Inc. at the time, rushed to the Barber's rescue.

HULKAMANIA RUNS WILD AGAIN AS HULK LIFTS THE CHAMPIONSHIP BELT INTO THE AIR FOR AN INCREDIBLE FIFTH TIME!

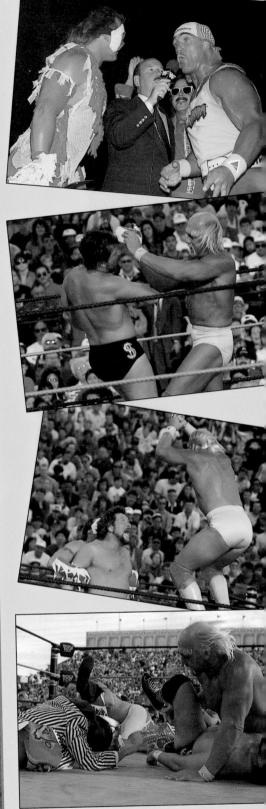

After the vicious attack, the Hulkster returned to ring action. The Mega-Maniacs battled Money Inc. for the Tag Team Belts at *WrestleMania IX*, but lost. However, later in the evening, the Hulkster entered the ring and defeated newly crowned Federation Champion Yokozuna to start his fifth title reign.

Steiner Brothers*

The Steiner Brothers, Rick and Scott, both excelled in amateur athletics such as wrestling and American football from grammar school through college. After graduating, these two big Michigan boys entered the professional wrestling ring. Then late last year they joined

the ranks of the World
Wrestling Federation.

Right away, the Steiners
clashed with another team
of brothers, the Beverlys.
Beau and Blake Beverly hail
from Michigan's neighboring
state of Ohio. However, the
Beverly Brothers were
raised very differently from
the Steiners. The Beverlys
were spoiled brats, used to
getting whatever they asked
for and wanted.

But the Steiners gave the
Beverlys what they didn't
want: big trouble. Look for
the Steiner Brothers to
make a run for the top of
the tag team ranks.

Bob Backlund*

With Bob Backlund, a former World Wrestling Federation champ, what you see is what you get. Returning to the ring after almost a decade, he remains the superb technician and the modest athlete that he has been ever since he first stepped onto a wrestling mat—or a football field.

Backlund really loves to wrestle. That's why he came back to the squared circle. That's also why he has spent years coaching young amateur wrestlers, trying to instill his strong sense of fair play and athletic competitiveness in them.

What lies ahead for Bob Backlund? Maybe glory. Maybe not. But, for him, just wrestling well is happiness—and he is a very, very happy man.

Bob Backlund

GAMES

CHAMPIONS

How much do you know about World Wrestling Federation Champions Hulk Hogan, Macho Man Randy Savage and Bob Backlund? There are three questions about each champion. Give yourself a point for correctly answering the first question, two points for answering the second and three for the third. If you score between 18-15, you're also a champ. Between 14-10, good going. If you get less than 10, you're missing a lot.

1 No one has held the World Wrestling Federation Title more than Hulk Hogan. How many times has he worn the belt?

2 Do you remember which opponent he beat for his first title?

3 Hulk won the title one time with the help of what unlikely accomplice, who brained his opponent with a chair?

1 Has Savage held any other titles during his years in the World Wrestling Federation? If so, which one(s)?

2 The Macho Man won an elimination tournament held at *WrestleMania IV* to become champion for the first time. Do you remember whom he beat in the finals of that competition?

3 Savage again won the belt at *WrestleMania VIII* when he defeated Ric Flair. His victory was somewhat tainted. Can you explain?

1 Backlund decries all the showmanship in wrestling. He regards the sport as what?

2 He was the World Wrestling Federation's longest-reigning champion. For how many years did he hold the title?

3 Backlund also co-held the Tag Team Title with what renowned wrestler?

Giant Gonzalez*

Giant Gonzalez, a huge, animalistic brute close to 8 feet tall, raged his way into the World Wrestling Federation at the *Royal Rumble* with a fury that shocked the world.

No one expected it. As the Undertaker cleaned house in the *Royal Rumble* battle royal, the Giant stalked to ringside, entered the squared circle and challenged the Undertaker.

Then he proceeded to do what no one before had ever done. With bestial fury, he beat the shocked Undertaker into unconsciousness, snarling

through it all the while.

The Giant was brought to the arena by the devious Harvey Wippleman, who detests the Undertaker. In the monster, Wippleman now has a wrestler who spreads fear throughout the entire ranks of the World Wrestling Federation.

During *WrestleMania IX*, the Giant pounded the Undertaker but could not put him away. Thwarted, the Giant put the Undertaker out with a sedative-soaked rag. Miraculously revived by his urn, the Undertaker attacked, and the Giant fled the ring.

GAMES

PERSONAL EFFECTS

Do you recognize the pictured items? Each is associated with a World Wrestling Federation superstar. First, fill in the owners' names. Then, take the letters in the boxes and unscramble them to come up with the answer to some grappling trivia.

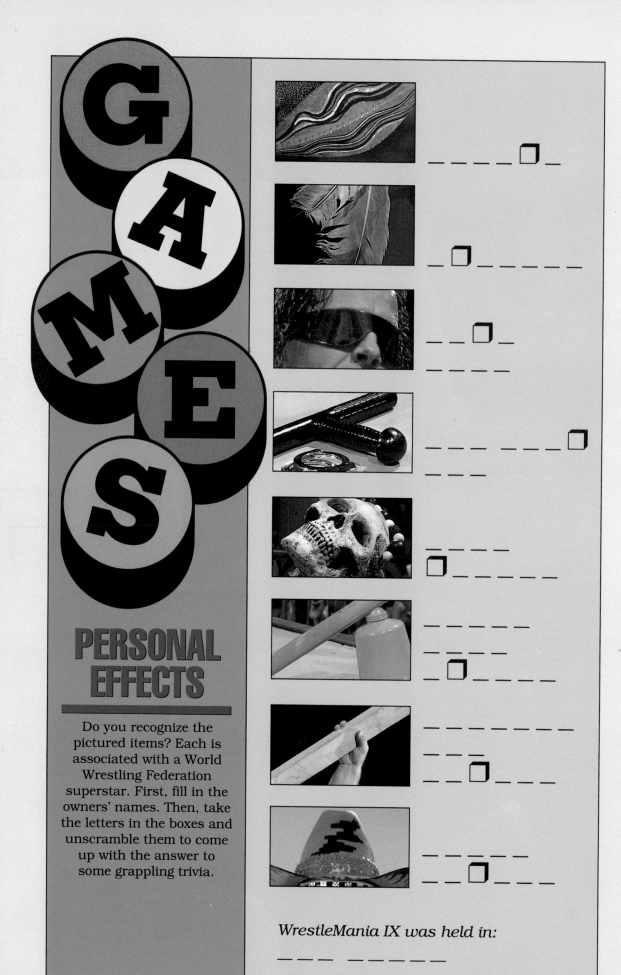

_ _ _ _ _ ☐ _

_ ☐ _ _ _ _ _ _

_ _ ☐ _

_ _ _ _ _ _ ☐
_ _ _

☐ _ _ _ _ _

_ _ _ _ _
_ ☐ _ _

_ _ _ _ _
_ _ ☐ _ _

_ _ _ _ _
_ _ ☐ _ _

WrestleMania IX was held in:

_ _ _ _ _ _ _ _ _

Kamala*

Kamala the Ugandan Giant lost his match against the Undertaker at the *Survivor Series*. But Kamala won his dignity. He is a simple man, but he finally recognized that his sneaky manager, Dr. Harvey Wippleman, and handler Kimchee were using him. Under the guidance of the Reverend Slick, Kamala developed a sense of dignity he never had before.

This does not mean that Kamala is less of a competitor in the ring. On the contrary, he is now more focused than before, able to utilize all of his tremendous physical attributes. Kamala is lucky. He has been given the chance to begin life anew.

Shawn Michaels*

Shawn Michaels made a number of people in the United Kingdom quite unhappy when he beat the British Bulldog for the World Wrestling Federation Intercontinental Title. Lots of people dislike Shawn. Sure, they recognize that he is a fantastic wrestler, but they don't cotton to his posturing and haughtiness.

His pride came down a notch or two when he lost to Champion Bret "Hit Man" Hart at the *Survivor Series*—but not for long.

Michaels then went after his former tag team partner, Marty Jannetty, to prove that he had carried the duo's matches in the past. Along the way, the proud Michaels lost his manager, Sensational Sherri, who could no longer tolerate his arrogant ways.

Sherri was vindicated at *WrestleMania IX* when a worried Shawn ensured his own disqualification against Tatanka by manhandling the referee. He lost the match but retained his belt.

Papa Shango*

The high priest of the dark side of voodoo, Papa Shango tried to put his curse on Bret "Hit Man" Hart, but he failed. That is one of his few failures in the World Wrestling Federation.

Shango has terrorized opponents, psychologically and physically. So very strong is his personality that his claims of sorcery have paralyzed numerous opponents. The few individuals who have managed not to flinch psychologically have all been crushed physically by Papa Shango's huge body and his dark power.

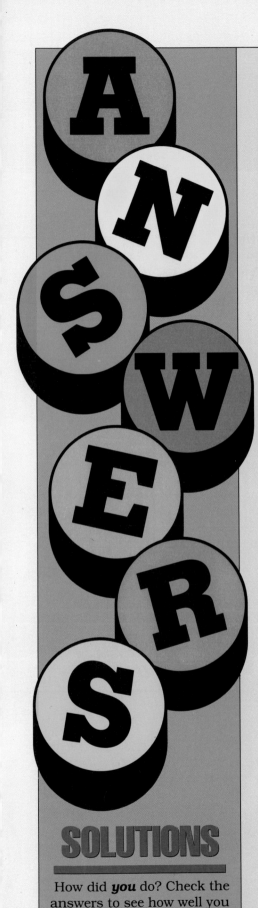

SOLUTIONS

How did **you** do? Check the answers to see how well you know the superstars of the World Wrestling Federation.

YOU'VE REALLY GOT A HOLD ON ME

The wrestlers and their moves are:
1. REVERSE FALLAWAY SLAM, **2.** BOSTON CRAB, **3.** TOMBSTONE, **4.** CRANIUM CRUNCH, **5.** COBRA CLUTH, **6.** SHOULDERBREAKER, **7.** SHARPSHOOTER, **8.** ELBOW OFF THE TOP ROPES, **9.** BACK SUPLEX, **10.** RUNNING CLOTHESLINE, **11.** CROWBAR LEG GRAPEVINE and **12.** FALLAWAY SLAM

BORN IN THE USA!

The correct combination is: **1.** Allentown, **2.** Minneapolis, **3.** Calgary, **4.** Shaker Heights, **5.** Sarasota, **6.** Venice Beach, **7.** Glens Falls, **8.** Charlotte, **9.** Norfolk, **10.** Death Valley, **11.** Cobb County and **12.** San Antonio

CHAMPIONS

The answers are: **HULK HOGAN**, five, the Iron Sheik and Ric Flair; **MACHO MAN RANDY SAVAGE**, yes, the Intercontinental Title, Ted DiBiase and he grabbed Flair's trunks sending him to the canvas for the pin; **BOB BACKLUND**, a science, six years, and Pedro Morales.

PERSONAL EFFECTS

The respective owners are (reading from top to bottom): KAMA**L**A, **TA**TANKA, BR**ET** HART, BIG BOS**S** MAN, PAPA **S**HANGO, MODEL RICK M**A**RTEL, HACKSAW JIM DU**G**GAN and RANDY SA**V**AGE.
WrestleMania IX was held in: **LAS VEGAS**.

OF MOUTH AND MEN

Jimmy Hart's champions are: **M**OUNTIE, BR**E**T HART, HONKY TONK **M**AN, TY**P**HOON, EART**H**QUAKE, TED D**I**BIASE and KNOBB**S** AND SAGS.
Hart was born in **MEMPHIS**.

Doink*

Doink is a sick, evil clown who truly enjoys playing very cruel tricks on people, especially children. One of his meanest tricks involved Crush, the big wrestler from Hawaii. Doink attacked Crush at ringside with a weighted artificial arm that the clown pretended was his own injured limb. Crush was hit so hard that he suffered a concussion.

But Crush recovered and met Doink at *WrestleMania IX*. Crush splattered the clown all over the ring, but Doink had more tricks up his sleeve. Under the ring, Doink had hidden another clown who looked just like him. At a pivotal point in the match, the referee was knocked out. The Doink double emerged, and the two clowns trashed Crush. When the referee awoke, he found Doink pinning Crush and declared him the winner. A second referee ran out and protested, but when the officials looked under the ring, the double was gone.